from the field book

Carol Thistlethwaite

BeWrite Books

The Select Six is as much a commisioning tool as a showpiece website for the best six poems most recently submitted.
Visit the Select Six at:
www.bewrite.net/select_six.htm

Published internationally by BeWrite Books, UK.
32 Bryn Road South, Wigan, Lancashire, WN4 8QR.

A CIP catalogue record for this book is available from the British Library

ISBN: 978-1-905202-76-8

Also available in eBook format.

Produced by BeWrite Books
www.bewrite.net

Illustrations © Tom Adamson

Cover photo by Chris Rae
based on a drawing by Tom Adamson

About the author …

I have only met Carol Thistlethwaite the once – when I did a reading in Liverpool's magnificent Library. I was already aware of her poetry through the small presses, and knew that she had read her poetry on Radio Lancashire and Radio Merseyside. I had previously published some of Carol's earlier works and had been impressed. Then I started to come across her bird poems …

So taken was I with this new direction of hers that whenever I saw that she was a contributor to a magazine hers were the first pages I turned to – to see what she had done this time to capture this avian essence, this jizz. She rarely failed me.

'Contributor's notes' informed me that Carol used to be a field teacher for the Royal Society for the Protection of Birds (RSPB). She has subsequently gained an MA (distinction) in Writing Studies and now helps others develop their skills in her role as creative writing tutor. Walker, writer, ornithologist – she loves it all and her enthusiasm is infectious.

Small wonder then that when I moved to Cumbria and had difficulty identifying the smaller estuary birds it was Carol I contacted first to ask her help. And small wonder too that when she submitted her bird poems to The Journal and to The Select Six website I jumped at the chance to publish them. And when she approached me regarding a collection of her bird poems … Well …

Carol now earns her living as a learning support tutor who empowers adults with physical, sensory, mental health and learning difficulties. In that role she promotes learning and helps people develop confidence and self-esteem. And in that capacity she is the author of three books for adults who are learning to read. This, however, is Carol's first single author poetry collection. I can only hope that her poems bring you as much pleasure as they've given me.

Sam Smith – 2008

Acknowledgements

Thanks to all the staff and volunteers at the RSPB Ribble Discovery Centre where I used to work. Special thanks to volunteers Pat Downey, Anne Freeman and the late Pat Few who often helped me to take school parties mud dipping there. Also to the RSPB, the Wildfowl and Wetlands Trust (WWT) and similar organisations whose reserves I have enjoyed visiting.

A special mention to Chorley Natural History Society and in particular Neil Southworth, Nora and Tommy West, Gary Lilley and David Beattie for welcoming me to monthly duck counts, walks, annual bird races and for sharing sightings.

I'd like to thank Sam Smith for his understanding of the jizz articulated in these poems and also for his final editing advice.

Some of these poems have previously been published singly and in groups in the following magazines, anthologies and websites: *Birds of Bowland, Carillon, Creature Features, Fire, The Frogmore Papers, The Journal, Listening to The Birth Of Crystals* (Paula Brown Publishing), *Look Out, Neon Highway, Poetry Cornwall, Poetry Monthly, The Select Six, The Penniless Press, The People's Poet, Reach* and *Weyfarers*.

To ornithologists everywhere and especially to those volunteers who cheerfully give their time and energy to promote and protect wildlife worldwide.

Contents

the jizz

split instant

place   sound
that wordless leap
from colour / shape
    movement

        to recognition
    jizz

Rowing in the Dawn

Sun stretches,
heaving up above the trees
as rowers pull across the lake
rumpling her rest.

Overhead
herons gently wake the breeze;
throats heavy with the unsung,
carry dreams
into a rising day.

Heron

away from
the shuddering hide

is a calm,
whose neck is hunched
and still

catkins snatched by the breeze
twigs ripped from birch

where wildness is diffused
through grey, white feathers

great grebe
make desperate dives
again again
into a ridging mere

solitary harpoon
remains poised
steady

jackdaws lift and land lift and
land unsettling wigeon whistles
as moorhens jerk red shields
into the folding waves

and still
the heron waits

Lapwings

early rays awake
the colours of the trees,
decrystallising oak,
and beech-hedge-tops
melt to glinting bronze,
and in the field
lapwing
statues
wait for day
to angle down,
their feet stuck to filigree,
crests flat,
plover beaks, all
paused,
for the muslin spread to fade,
and for feet and beaks to sink
into a soft brown thaw

9th December 2005, Rufford

Snipe

harder than a jigsaw
matching reeds
this standing back
and straining with binoculars
for a slim brush of movement,
the contra comb of feathers,
waiting,

waiting,
wondering
if there really are any there,
and if one or more will ever step out
from such a snug dimension

                                    in   i

        shots   t
   eyes,   s
      breath,
   towing   w
     away,
    zagging   a
      zig-
    second
  a split
   then-   k
at you,
  startling
 heel-shock-deep   e
 rip from rest.
  sudden-
   ...until there's a
   a field.
    middle of
  right across the
 of seep-in puddles
sinking trails
and stubble roots,
  in dark earth
   gun boots squelching
    is walking into wind,
   he said
    The best way,

snipe

Curlews

April gurgles through the moor
as winter weeps away,
and curlews wake the rising springs
with curving beaks,
both burbling again.

Avocet

straw-bent-legs   stylish curves
black piped on white   neat   no waste
minimalist dream

Greenshank

solitary, downward-looking, high-stepping,
ankle-bending, green-legged stalker-walker,
    up-beaked prober of the shallow pool

    then – a fleeting movement instigates a
        bursting into splasher   –
                      fisher   –
                            dasher –
                        twisting
           energetic stabbing-plashing
                          after
                  quick-flick
                              fry

Marshside, Southport

Oystercatchers

Conspicuous,
black and white,
at low-tide
– oystercatchers.
On pink legs,
with toes spread,
long red beaks
probe the mud
for shells.
Thick and strong, their beaks
prise macoma, hammer cockles open.
Handsome, noisy predators:
no need for camouflage.

Oystercatchers

oystercatchers taste bad

confident in their invulnerability

a giant brash butterfly
of inky-black and white
with a slash of red

the place rings
to the incomparable piping
and *kleep*ing

intense sound
transports me

this is life
being lived

Taken, with thanks, from Rob Hume: 'A Bank Too Far', Birds, Winter 2006

Redshank

Light on feet,
probing prettily
with the tip of beak.
Quick stepper of the mud,
run, run, stab,
run, run, stab,
to life's rapid beat,
darting
with her long, red legs,
to the sound
of corophium-seek.

Redshank at St Annes

sun softens
sinking in surrender
to a wide awaiting sea,
as redshank ripple rings,
orange legs glisten,
give themselves to be
        translucent,
beaks flick briny drops,
toss concentric dance,
parting beaks
lunge the estuary for more,
reflections,
redshank above
redshank below
near perfect symmetry,
movement, rhythm,
        meltdown,
pouring peach pink gold,
tide withdraws,
follows fallen star,
silvered afterglow,
redshank silhouettes
secret witnesses,
feed on

Turnstone

chink plink chink plink pebble-flipping-turnstone flicking over stones, salted orange legs, shingle-clitter-claws, beaks tipped to speculate tide's tonguing of the shore licking colours into pebbles richer than before. Tiny flick-pickers, flock on the move, feathers flecked with speckles from beaches they have known.

Knot

Winter orb's
reflected splendour
spreads across the flat expanse
to where a group of knot
stout, unhurried
probe the mud.   *Through*
their midst dunlin
prick a thread of running stitch,
small, vivid dark on light,
shallow peckers darting on.

Alarm

draws-up-flock-of-silhouettes,
gathered-in-knot-fly-as-one,
glint-to-white
dip-back-to-black,
diamond-flash
farewell,

day slips its crown into the sea,
seeps mud with majesty.

Sanderlings

On the beach – faded waders:
six weeks of courtship's colour,
bonding, mating, rearing – done
and gone. Now their feathers wear the Arctic wind,
colours pushed to spangled greys,
snow bellies, matchstalk legs
strike out at break-neck speed,

their high-cute factor, hard as quartz,
their sooty legs, strong as jet,
their wave-chase games, ruthless as a tungsten beak,
each a tundra surface melt,
each a survivor, full of pretty flowers,
with permafrost beneath.

27th September 2007, Rossall Point

Water Rail

Her slender hips
that slip through stems with grace,
now hesitate,
she tests the open space with an elegant toe,
pauses

– nothing stirs,
so she cautiously begins to emerge,
her shy demeanour
discomforted
by risking exposure.
This sylphlike creature,
with spinster-thin red beak
and suppressed, yet stylish dress,
delicately picks her way across the gap,
quietly focuses on the next patch of plants,
the next hiding place,
and wasting no time her prim poise retires
from view again.

And what a surprise, to later hear her
squealing, loud and wild,
like a harlot of the night,
from somewhere deep in the safety
of a dense, reedy bed.

Moorhens

Impertinently close,
  instant scrapping over scrapes,
    scudding scuffle,
      sculpting necks
        squall
          into a squabble.
  Sculling feet-attack,
          grappling yellow toes,
flap-thrust from the water
            to pin and push opponent down,
                      threaten
                      drown.
    Scrimmage, squawk, scuffle,
        splashing scruples, scrubbing out,
        leaping over
        head.
  Squaring shields, red-to-red,
    brassy beak-tips craning low,
      tibias tilting, rears raising,
    wings arc in high dudgeon
      to hurl the last *kurr'uk*.

Tail feathers rise and fan
      displaying haughty-white,
          slow now, self-conscious turn,
        he squires-off with swagger,
      defiance glaring from the white-flag
          feather-flashing by his bum....

Drake-Rape

Mallard,
limp and neck down:
how many tried
and exhausted her
to drowning?
Four, five, six at a time?
Eager to fertilise:
instinct to drake-rape.

Adrift,
alone in a corner
where waste gathers:
Ribena carton – emptied and crushed,
green foil crisp bag – discarded,
spent feathers,
used, screwed up then thrown away.
Drake-raped.

On the nearest island,
in the nest from which she was chased,
a clutch of ten, greenish white eggs,
covered with down from her breast,
await
nothing.

Drake-rape.

Fairhaven Lake, Lytham St Annes

Cygnets

Half a dozen bob
in little halos,
pearly grey heads,
round, black teddy eyes
and charcoal beaks.
They float like dandelion clocks
with tiny beads of water
sparkling on their backs.

The cob's orange beak
patrols from side to side,
high head, half-open wings,
watching for the hour
when seeds are blown away
from the shadow of his whiteness
to a lightness of their own.

Crèche

Seventy goslings
quickly and quietly
marshalled across the lake
by ten Canada geese.
Each youngster flips its flat and floppy feet
clown-like up the slope,
then toddles to a lawn
cushioned with daisy dwarfs,
where they nestle down,
fuzzy, silver-brown
nudging necks to tug the grass
from a June afternoon.

Fairhaven Lake, Lytham St Annes

Pink-footed Geese

Compass-needle-necks
fly in billow-arrowheads,
bracing breezes from the North
homing into Ribble's waiting weeds.
Skeins level-up for landings,
slip through slits of light,
break rank
heels down
adjusting final flaps.
They pack the base, squadron
after squadron after
squadron emerge
from soft brown dusks,
racing sunsets.
Drakkar necks raid,
feast with Nordic gaggle,
part-time settlers
quilt the estuary, bedding down,
till warmer nights
leave lovers cold each spring.

Martin Mere WWT

Shelduck

<pre>
          big duck
        high and dry
          stilted
          on pink
           legs

         flat wet mud
          neck dips
      black head, coral bill
     sweep from side-to-side
        slow advance
  vacuum-suck-and-sieve-hydrobia
          leave behind
      web

              -
                 z
                     i
                         g
                             -
                                        web
  -    g   n   i   g   g   a   z
     b
             e
                   a
                       k
                                   -
      web   s
                              c
                         r
                   a
          p
     e
</pre>

Night Roost

They reel, higher, lower,
higher, lower, not yet ready to roost
upon this lake of concertinas,
and when a few descend, the others draw them up again,
circling, searching for a place.

It's not just black-headed gulls wintering tonight –
but lesser black-backs, too, are seeking
shelter from a wind that's bullying the clouds
and riding roughshod down the hills.
Six cormorants dash north, towards Anglezarke,
a small group of gulls peels itself way,
uncertainty racing east against the bruising light ,
as the rest hastily land, invisible now,
where white horses canter, working up to a gallop
as the storm bares its teeth, ready to bite.

13th January 2007, Lower Rivington Reservoir

black-headed gulls

seize it quick wing away
pursued by many more   tw
                              is
                    ti
                        ng, tilt   the
                                   ing in   air
                                             holding tight
                                          every gull for himself

                                             loose scrum
                                                drop

                                             splash

                                             dive

                                          back in play
        attempt a try
                              maul
                    call
                 all
hungry for conversion

Cemlyn Bay

Just one of those evenings
when mist holds the setting sun,
subdues it to an April linnet's blush,
just one of those dusks
that levels the sea so we can watch
seven merganser arc and dive,
just one of those calm times
when the shingle wants to tuck our toes into its bed,
tell us breathe more slowly,
and listen to each tern softly rustle down
on the islet of sleep, where plover already rest
with feather over beak,
just one of those moments when we feel eyelids flicker
just before we drop –

then bolt awake
    as tern-plover jerk
  and cry *alarm*,
rise as one, filter into types,
the golden plovers' tight-packed ranks
      steer sharp left,
sharp right, black bellies sweep across our sight, flick
to streak dark gold across the night,
as sandwich terns *kik, kik* themselves higher, higher
in the sky, above the kestrel's hover,
until they nudge this fear from their rest,
as day's retina starts to close, slowly mutes the bay
to a pale rosy-grey, and stilled wings
once again steady the pending night.

12th April 2007

Sandwich Tern

spiked back,   just back
    the windborne look,
  claiming stretches of the islet
in the brackish lagoon,
a noisy bunch, they
guard the shore with gull and golden plover,
        slicker than the black-heads,
            wings elbowing for space. And already
males are flying in with gifts of eels for mates
who have no time to waste.

11th April 2007, Cemlyn Bay

Common Tern

Such eloquence,
a poised question mark
dips to dot its point,
pricks a lively fish
from the shallowest of pools,

black-headed gulls crowd in,
over-dipped in ink,
web-feet-first,
blotting the page,

the tern returns,
watches from the breeze,
full stops another,

the gulls shrug their wings,
smudge their images.

Solway

Gannets off Bass Rock

Circling higher,
seeing further,
deeper,
gannets prey on fish
where a would-be king hunted heir to throne.

Precision dives fracture sea,
threaten skulls,
harpooning plunders plosh.

Birds and men, both
spear for survival,
taking captives back to Bass
to secure the future of their lines.
Arrows are propelled by strings
taut for survival.

Years ago monks would harry bird,
eat young flesh, eggs,
sell its oil for the Vatican,
whose sole purpose is to fish.

Now peaceful
men withdraw from Bass,
circle higher,
looking further, deeper
as the gannets do.

Bass Rock, now a seabird sanctuary, is situated three miles east of Berwick, Scotland and has been used as a refuge, religious retreat and political prison throughout its stormy history.

.

Gannets

... leaning into sand dunes,
warmth moulding to our backs,
we lazily watch wavelets
crest turquoise in the sun,
splutter along their ridges
to collapse, whitening the beach,

and as we drift our gazes towards the gentle breeze,
we notice gannet-crosses flash white against blue,
solos,
and groups cascading
at ninety, sixty, thirty degrees,
inverting dives with fountains
splashing high against the sky,
as birds power down
into a slick-silver world,

and trawling through their midst,
two red and white fishing boats,
labouring the swell,
working their way to an uncertain North Sea,

and last night's salted cod and chips,
steaming from white paper,
flaking in my fingers,
vinegar on tongue,
now seems
far too easy for me

13th August 2007, Fraserburgh Bay

43

Gannets and Great Skuas

They patrol the coast,
dark shadows that take you by surprise
even though you know they're there – somewhere.
They appear suddenly from nowhere,
bad memories that strike from behind,
knock the stuffing from you,
steal your sustenance;
or sometimes they sidle up
in the corner of your eye,
circle your resistance,
menace your resolve to hold on tight,
forcing you down
until you relinquish the fish, your dream,
and are left to start diving all over again.

Stromness

Fulmar

Now they have the cliffs all to themselves,
empty are the thin ledges where kittiwake bustled and balanced,
where guillemots and razorbills held tight,
now they have it all, these plump Fulmar chicks,
dozing in peace or rasping for more,
as they fill out the plush upper cliffs,
single chicks,
waiting for their stiff-winged parents
working hard to spoil them with fish, squid
and yet more fish.

Eider Duck

here, where flagstone rocks obstruct the tide,
make it curl, crash and foam,
where brine is churned to frothy scum
and torn kelps scent the breeze,
where bone would crack and keratin snap
is where mothers with their young,
and males in eclipse
choose to rest:
islets of calm,
where duck, wrack, rock
merge into one

Brough Sound, Orkney

shags

they criss the bay,
wings brushing waves,
straight-necked messengers
homing onto these flat rocks,
that slip their past towards the sea,
like pages from spineless books,
words washing free,

it's here they land – shake – preen,
pose with lectern-wings,
I wonder what they mean
as they

transform to slender bottles
(unseen messages inside),
then drop themselves into the ocean,

necks like periscopes,
they aim towards a patch of calm
splash salty water over backs,
dip heads and necks into the swell,
shake it through –
then suddenly they're run, run, running over water,
flapping into silent flights,
trailing white stepping stones
which vanish
as each achieves the air,

missionaries
crossing the sound,
with wings brushing waves

Brough Sounds, Orkney

47

Guillemot

They nest on dimples of ledge,
claw tips curled round nodules of rock,
beaks up like spires,
minding and voicing everyone's business,
sheltering their young from a perilous fall
with a single row of feathers,
enduring
the stench,
guano drying on their heads,
until a partner returns with offerings
of a break: a flight to wash
and feed.

This is the struggle,
the price of the way,
colonising a cliff
with an instinct to cling,
knowing that even here, one freak wave
could wipe a season's work away.

July 2006, Fowlsheugh

Cormorants

Cretaceous remnants, perhaps,
long shadows of an era,
whose outspread wings
and serpent necks
gather up the sunlight,
to see them through
another age of darkness.

Noontide

From dense cloud to marshy ground, this whole place is heavy with suspense. The suspense that precludes a spectacle of uncertain certainties. A spectacle when nothing, not the vapour in the air, not the droplets in the sea, knows how far the tide might reach, how far its ripples might edge into and over it, steadily and unstoppably through its channels, through its stems, to smother it as smoothly and seamlessly as silk. Nothing knows for sure which bank or patch of marsh might remain uncovered by the slowly coming tide or which high ground might escape predatored blood. It's not just the waders and the gulls, the passerines, too, bunch up with their kindred: collared doves cling to a barn roof together, starlings huddle on communication wires. Curlews have already abandoned the coast; they stand camouflaged in fields. Lapwings and their golden cousins snuggle there too and tucked in tight between them, ringed plover also hide. Out on the mud, there's a coalition-truce. The great black-backs have stopped their bullying and quietly join ranks with lesser black-backs, herring and black-headed gulls, who watch their young, who all watch the tide. Suddenly a small platoon of shelducks rises and deserts the tidal line, leaving only oystercatchers to bolster a defence. Further up the coast, retreating waders fly in flocks; leggy godwits abandon bastions to advancing waves. Now oystercatcher-banner after oystercatcher-banner begin to withdraw, each troop streaming longer as the onslaught presses in. Whole armies of dunlins are now on the run, beating as one, as they change their formations, twisting and turning in and out of sight. And finally, the tide has reached the peak of its invasion, has spread itself too thin, pauses, before gathering itself and shrinking back to bulk the open sea.

And it's only now that we notice monotone grey plover, who have held their ground, who have stood it out near the estuary mouth, each solitary soldier on its own tussock of grass, islanded and insular, each one holding on.

And now as the tide retreats, herons start to emerge from the shelter of fields, start to grab the spoils of the push, the straggling fish that are getting left behind, that are trying to escape the battled ground.

And as the afternoon starts to thin, the sun makes little skips on skimming water and a blue sky starts to reappear.

13th September 2007, Pilling Sands

Black-tailed Godwits

No matter how cold the water, wind,
day or night, they're in,
belly-deep-in
survival,
beaks, heads, necks shouldering down,
working the mud,
balancing worms, shake-by-shake,
along narrow beaks, down the warmth of the throat.

Then they rest, chests into the breeze,
feeling it push and flatten feathers to skin.

Marshside, Southport

Stonechat

he assumes his pose
on his limelight stone,
rich, brown, velvet head,
white shoulder fleck,
chattering on about his life,
importanting himself,
claiming his space,

he repeats from the stage stone wall,
then a bracken head,

from time-to-time she chatters back,
from the middle of the bracken,
her drabber dress wearing thin,
her wings rolled up – telling their offspring what to do

Stronstrey Bank, Anglezarke

Garden on a Winter's Day

A goldcrest semi-quavers twig-to-twig
in piccolo staccatos.

Goldfinch arrive in the tinkling of bells:
paired faces glow astride the nyger feeder.

The robin soloist begins.

Two greenfinch suddenly sheer up like cymbals
clashing at each other in vertical dispute.

A timpani of long-tailed tits bounce in
like happy ping-pong balls,
providing light percussion from the black-budded ash.

Steely-backed nuthatch whistles in like a flute,
wing-flutters at the edge of sight
to scatter great tits from the feeder.

Wren plucks spiders' harps along the top of the fence,
dunnock shies away from the stage,
follows the score by shaking beech leaves
from the base of the hedge,
both keeping sight of the magpie at the podium.

A jay starts scolding from the nearby oak,
reveals blue flashes, but to no avail–
three grey squirrels break in anyway,
scamper through the set,
tip over music stands,
and within the next minim–
the symphony has fled.

Starlings

first a small group
then another, and another
move across a space,
groups grouping
merging into single-consciousness,
patterns, sounds
easing in and out of forms:
crescents, spheres, tears
traced onto indigo,
they submerge me now,
seem to threaten my existence:
swooping low,
darkening the sky,
listen, watch, be,
peeling off their indistinctness,
dropping down in lines,
phonemes raining,
pouring
just beyond my reach

Starlings

Moon-rushed tide shoving in, breeze pushing out,
waders crowd receding habitat
where predators cramp-in: merlin, peregrine
flushing out, twanging up bowls of starling dust,
lapwing vortex in the azure like heavy sediment,
as starlings filter through, elongate, straining into
waves: front half thrusting forward, rear dragging back,
a stretch of wills that almost comes unthread.
In these uncertain days of summer skies and autumn rains,
the heavy-fronted mass sinks to meadow grass,
stragglers towed down to ground, not quite able to repel
gravitation to their murmeration.

Redwing

I heard of them in Juniors:
how they flew from other places,
wintered here. I never saw one
on my way to school.

Now I see them everywhere, flocks
of silhouettes, rising from the fields,
striping hawthorn bare.

The mistle thrush, however, was never
unaware. Rattling from a berry bush,
he's seen it all before:
white spring confetti,
a summer snatching seeds,
waiting for the berry-swell,
blush and then the migrant rush,
wafting in, thousands feasting
on the husbandry of the native species.

Blackbird

where foxgloves spire up
chiming pink incense,

and where streams dance over pebbles
in diamanté royal trains,

and where the sun unfolds its glory
as rainbows release life,

and where trees wave their welcome banners
as the breeze rushes through,

is where blackbird shares the kingdom
and crowns it with his psalm

House Sparrow

It feels soooo good,
this scritch of grit on belly skin,
scrubbing it in, scratching the chin,
grovelling in the gravel,
scraping wings in dust, carding feathers' grain,
again, again,
scooping it, flicking it, catching the scratch on its back,
raking the particle-power,
shaking from crown down to tail,
edging it through,
feeling the pumice pick,
cleansing, de-miting,
tingling soooo fine!

Wren

– a chuck of tiny clockworks,
all chirring coils and springs,
fully wound, brand new from the box,
single tail feathers hastily stuck on at ninety degrees.

Their outsized wiry feet grab at twig and trunk,
or push-trip through the grass,
where parents hush their yellow stutters,
silence them with grubs,
acutely aware
that this excited break-out
is more fragile than eggs.

30th May 2007, Mere Sands

Pied Wagtails

Now the bell has rung
they claim the playground for themselves,
running, bobbing, nodding heads,
picking up down-trodden things,
inspecting gritty patches
where spilt drinks attract flies,
this emptied place – a feast
in foot-printed waste.

Robin

British Bulldog,
Defender of its territory,
Reliant,
Face of Christmas cards,
Winter's rosy cheer,
Resilient songster of the cold months,
Initiator of the woodland chorus,
Closer of the garden vesper,
Commonplace,
Undervalued,
A spade handle
– worth polishing.

Upon a Crow

overhanging branch

sudden
sheet blindness
(sun off water
fills the path)

caw
carrion-clean-carcass

dark
ragged
flaps
into
brightness

Kestrel and Crow

The morning clouds are pushing
each other for space,
a crow holds his shadow
over a chestnut feathered back,
swooping, twisting, imposing on,
disrupting the chase,

and as the kestrel scoops low,
I would lose him
against the rush-and-bracken-hill,
except that his crow-shadow
tracks him right across the moor.

5th September 2007, White Coppice

Rooks

It seems the wildest place to build
nests,
in the tops of tallest trees.

Way below shine celandine,
where soleprints linger
moist for months,
sheltered,
in the patterning of shade.

But oh to be up there!
To know the thrash and thwack
of life all-precarious.
Sticks, accidentally dropped, are
lost, gone, discarded.
Fate.
Rooks never waver to retrieve.

Jays

today their wings dig the air
with purpose

discarded are their leafy cloaks
of shyness

today they're out in numbers
out in the open

bold blue flashing through the oaks
as moustached beaks pluck acorn after acorn

white-rumping them across the open sky
to the thin forest edge

where they stash them
under newly falling leaves

some to be retrieved at the hungry edge of winter
others left to thicken the receding forest's reach

7th October 2007, White Coppice

Chough

for Les

Oh happy chough,
soaring memories of childhood days
and acrobatic play,
trampolining beds
and reckless fold-wing dives.
You open up a dressing box,
recall the clomp of red high heels
tripped by feet too small,
and practice lipstick smears,
wrapped in a big black shawl.
Those pointed-finger wings
Of witchlike silhouette,
veer down a memory
of curl-edged story books,
and leave us now to hanker
for innocent chough-filled days.

Brambling

Blue tits and great tits decorate the wood
by looping living streamers through the birch,
while chaffinch wings shake flecks of artificial snow
throughout the lower boughs and undergrowth.
And see – their streaky cousins have arrived for the season,
russet-shouldered, plumping up the woodland's floor,
snacking on the beech mast as they go.

8th December 2006, Grey Heights

Nuthatch

for Wez

Announcing himself,
sleek whistler of the woods,
a whole slice of cool!
flexing his spine, concave and convex,
master of the bough,
simply upping it,
then upside-downing it,
headfirsting his descent,
the one and only –
adroit acrobat,
poised on the side of a trunk,
whooping it up
in elegant grey and stylish buff,
the showman of the wood!

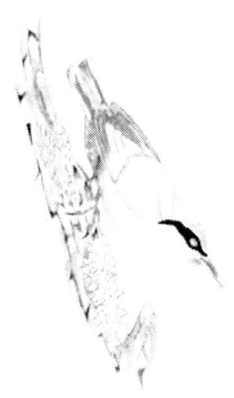

Treecreeper

… grip ground,
stock still,
waiting for the hack
and flick of plaque
to chisel open gaps,
as tiny curling claws
feather up a trunk,
soft underbelly,
cold, surgical sharp steel
prizes buried bugs,
chipping with precision,

the next customer …

Woodpigeon

a plump and pastel cushion
high up in the oak,
watches
  chaffinch flutter   in and
   out   of glistening baby leaves
              and a   robin rattle   through,
        random scatterings of   drops
whilst he just snuggles up,
loosened collar cooing sweetly to his mate
until the field dries

Swallows

for Jane

With a glide and a flutter they land
on telephone wires. Excited chatter.
Saharan sun-scorched faces,
grass-dust and salt-spray still fresh on bellies,
they thirst to procreate.
Before phones ever ring
they know
when the feet of flies tickle English celandines,
and wings beat,
butterflying north,
tracing the curves of Earth,
weaving lovers' lace
through the skies.
And as violets rush to colour
swallows sweep to barns,
build, rebuild their nests,
hatch, feed, fledge
the returning pulse of life.

Swallows

Scalloping low,
tweezering flies
at harvest time,
strength
for that dark-winged journey
of tail-streaming flight,
sleekness,
all pared down to
instinct.

Ankle-deep, I
squelch through dreams
rotting underfoot.

Swifts

for Alan

Urgent fledglings
drop
from nests,
beat the breeze
and thrust away
to Ethiopian Dreams.
'Onwards,'
the instinctive scream
to hills unseen,
this charge through life,
this racing on
even as they sleep.
And when they reach
the promised land,
there is no rest,
they fly the same,
each one driven,
corded to its kind.

Dipper

How do reedy legs and feathers
withstand the river's rush?
White chin squaring up
to a summer flood,
or charge of melted snow.
No matter. Unperturbed
it holds its own,
focused on a spot,
inspecting the outpour
like a master, not holding up the dash to class,
but savouring its energy,
then whirring back along the watercourse,
to chivvy everything into place.

Grey Wagtail

flashing yellow, splashing white,
she peaks and troughs,
peaks and troughs,
alights upon a stone,
refracting ripples bob, bob, bobbing
by her tail

Skylark

sheers up vertical,
flutters on a joyful chord,
tossing song
across the moor

Pipits and Larks on Heapey Moor

Up here, among heather, bilberry
and cotton grass, are little brown streaky birds,
white-tail-edged ascenders
towing songs,

thin pipits, undulate ribbons of peeping
calls, flitting over Roman walls.

And round bellied larks
tie opulent bows of thrilling trills,
then pull them tightly down
to ground.

Both gift wrapping wind and sky
in sweeps of spiral sound.

31st May 2007

Little Brown Jobs

A clifftop walk, rough pasture on the landward side,
at first I thought twite: small groups bursting up
then disappearing, always over shallow crests of land;
then binoculars allow a grey head, streaky back –
linnet, still pale before the ripening
of the strawberry breeding season.

And another group with white outer tails: pipit?
skylark? Not hovering on silver song today
but flitting low over fields then landing to feed.

And this one there's no mistaking:
greyish back, buff below – the wheatears have returned.
Perching on a stump, pale stripe above its eye,
and the *follow-me* rump flashing white
as it flits, flits, flits to an always-further-post.

12th April 2007, Church Bay to Porth y Bribys

Twite

a bunch bursts from the marsh,
white wing-flashes swirling round,
bound with elastic calls: *twe*it,
*twe*it, dropping down below the aster,
lower than the faded pink,
deep within the arrow grass,
tangling with the meadow mass,
in prostrate spurrey, they're in no hurry
where wind and rain fail to breach
and food is rich …

leaving me to wait,
and wait,
until
their next eruption

Whitethroat

whole-bodied launch
from top of hawthorn spike,
tail flicking,
head cresting,
throat back wide,
unashamedly, unhamperedly
true to himself

Grasshopper Warbler et alia

Such a tease! Prolong song
of clacker chatter reeling
me in, like a fish on a line,
towards some brambled mass,
where I can only stop-watch-listen,
wait, for
     a flick–
      dash
     into an even thicker thicket.
And as I turn, his stuttered clacker chatter
starts winding me again,

a whitethroat, too, flirts with me,
larking in the field of rape,
chuck-a-ro-che chuck-a-ro,
seven notes to look at me,
before my undulating dance
dips down into the stems
of oil seed, just low enough
to hide my high-rounded head,

and all the while
reed buntings, male,
perch, patiently on yellow spires,
constant songs,
black-hooded monks, white-banded napes, wait,
steadying my faith.

5th May 2007, Croston Marsh

Green Woodpecker

She feeds on the forest floor,
a dusty old lady in faded green frock.
But when she senses a presence –

she flies –
like a cabinet unfolding,
inside bright as yesterday,
and her laugh
so clear,
still here, today.

6th July 2007, Black Coppice

Green Woodpecker

Not like a bird at all
– this stump-legged
red-headed forager
of the forest floor.
This rooter of ants.

Alert as always,
he rises at my thoughts,
meets my expectations
in bright undulating swoops,
then hides himself away
from my critic's eye.

willow warbler

hu-eet
hop ***hu-eet***
leaves fluttering *flit-shadow* ***hu-eet***
flutteringleaves *hop flank* leavesfluttering
flutteringleavesflutteringtwig *flank shadow* leavesfluttering
flutteringleavesbranchflutteringleaves *hop tail* ***hu-eet*** leaves
flutteringleavesbranchflutteringleaves *flit shadow* leaves
flutteringleavesbranchflutteringleaves *shadow flit* fluttering
flutteringleavesbranchflutteringleaves *head flit* fluttering
flutteringleavesbranchflutteringleaves *hop tail* leaves
flutteringleavesbranchflutteringleaves ***hu-eet*** *flit tail* fluttering
flutteringleavesbranchflutteringleaves *willow* leaves
flutteringleavesbranchflutteringleaves *warbler* leaves
flutteringleaves *back flit* flutteringleaves
flutteringleavesbranchfluttering ***hu-eet*** *shadow* branchfluttering
flutteringleavesbranchfluttering *willow* branchandflutteringleaves
flutteringleavesbranchfluttering *warbler* branchandflutteringleaves
flutteringleavesbranchfluttering *flitting* branchandflutteringleaves
flutteringleavesbranch *further* branchandflutteringleaves
flutteringleavesbranch *back* branchandflutteringleavesbranch
flutteringleaves ***hu-eet*** *into* branchandflutteringleaves
flutteringleavesbranch the branchandflutteringleavesbranch
flutteringleavesandbranchandflutteringleaves

Meadow Pipits

When the moor still lies
in the cold sweat of sleep,
and hawthorn berries are not yet awake,
and meadow grass is swamped
by dream-drops,
it is the light chiming of pipits
that lifts the morning mist,
sweetens the air,
and wakens the words on my lips.

5th September 2007, White Coppice

Red-legged Partridge

There!
Two crouching heads,
stripes just visible above the grass,
then – bottlenecked stress,
suddenly fountains up – and runs
cartoon-like. Throats taut,
pushing past the field,
rushing past the panic panicking itself.

Kingfisher

I walk this stretch hoping for a gift
of turquoise breeze,
a lustrous fan full of wildness,
worth more than polished amber,
more than enamelled sky,
for the thrill of its elusiveness,
its independent streak,
known only to itself
when it will show. Hide.
Show itself again,
pulsing minnow-flash to feathers,
and always maintaining its wonder-at-me distance,
only revealing its shyest-best,
in case I value it less
for the close-up stench
of fish-gut
in its breath.

Kingfisher

a turquoise shimmer low-levels the bank. Pauses.

viridian resting on a shady branch
(unseen) had we not watched it land.

Then off again, quivering cerulean, until it stops
on a stump, burnt umber / lamp black.
the boldness of the breast defies vermilion and lemon
with a dot of yellow ochre?
How to leave a chin white and balance the weight of that
grey/black beak?
And how to record the watchful,

quiet plop

followed by a shaking up of spectrums
splattering water
adding prussian blue, sap green, replenishing
and diminishing
the water
content

Hen Harrier

for Luke

glorious abandon,
the black and white of it,
life tipped with death,
gushing down,
twisting into
skull split-timing,
sheer up
shimmer corkscrews to the sun,
arcing back-
breaking flips over the breeze,
to plummet
into daring glitter-spins,
defying swoop
breast brushing heather,
rocket up,
sudden stall,
fall,
yaw,
banking back for
harem's
applause

pipit clenches
flies in beak
darting deeper
in the moor

Kestrel

Fighting to remain
perched upon the breeze,
tail fanned so wide
each feather silhouettes.
Hunger hunting
eyes cut the frosty marsh,
focussed like a scimitar,
razored as the air.

Teamwork

```
i
 n
  t
   e
    r
     c
      e
       p
        t
         i
```
equal 100 kph flat race, peregrine chases pige**on**

                             peregrines
                               eat

Merlin

when flocks flutter,
stutter the
sky,
you know she's there,

when grass gasps,
crouching unease,
you know she's somewhere   there,

she holds your breath
as you scan the scene
for a dot in the sun,
a pause on a post,
talons clasp the beat of a heart,
future and past are scratched on an eye,
as feather and bone shake,
evaporate

Marshside, Southport

Barn Owl

for Ruth

furtive,
at the edge of consciousness,
this apparition of dusk,
cloaking wings,
enormous head and talons-spread search along the hedge
where misguided fears feel safely tucked
under thorns,

it quarters,
worrying the night,
silent as death,
reflecting what little is left of the day,
it drops
from sight,

then rises,
a phantom with the weight of life
hooked in its claws,
a last breath,
a last thought stolen
incomplete

Owl-light

Darkness falls,
wafting open quiet worlds
where fear stalks,
and moon's hushes pluck silvered webs,
ensnaring lullabies,
half calming, half guiding
predators,
through a place
where the shadow of an owl pierces the mouse.

For the twitcher whose name she never asked

Not quite summer, not quite autumn,
not a full moon tide, nor an offshore gale,
just a chance meeting on the marsh,
strangers sharing sightings,
a short-eared owl, trailing but not taking, a stirring flock of twite,
a skylark hesitantly taking a late season chance to sing,
enjoyed from a makeshift seat of plywood,
uncertainly
balanced on an estuary bank,
neither gazing at the other, binoculars scanning the bay,
talking about favourite local patches, and a fondness
for Italian restaurants.

Also published by the Select Six

The Way Back: Beyond Suburbia
by Nana Ollerenshaw

From the underbelly of the world, poems of a nurse, a trekker and a traveller.

Nana's poetry is perceptive of human nature, the land she has come to love, its shores and its wildlife. Her poems say 'take a closer look, adopt a sharper angle' – an angle that gives her work strength and insight. *Ron Wiseman*

A collection of gentle, reflective poems that explore aspects of the poet's life, work and everyday environment. They reveal an eye for detail, as well as great sensitivity to the subject. Her use of imagery delights. *Helen Gould*

This is a great little poetry book. Don't try to read it on the bus going to work with people bumping and pushing. Don't try to read it when you go to bed with sleep stealing in. You need to have your senses all to yourself, awake and alert, fully capable of absorbing the images and emotions … Read slowly, enjoy. *Stephen Reilly*

I enjoy these deceptively simple poems more as I read them. The occasional two line rhyme integrates and gives a sense of completion. The poems are cracks through which we glimpse the mystery of the natural world, the mystery of people and place. Though sometimes unsettling, they have the effect of re-affirming life. *Helen Hand*

Nana Ollerenshaw is essentially an acute observer. She reveals the intricacies of the relationships which she finds in the world around her, with a sharp eye, and illustrates them with an impressive, yet controlled, use of imagery. She seems always to strike the right note, to use the right word, without giving any sense of striving for effect. Her poetry is replete with insights, sometimes disturbing, sometimes humorous, but always humble, sensitive and appealing with their freshness. *Ken Pope*

ISBN 978-1-905202-20-1

Select Six
www.bewrite.net/select_six.htm

Also published by the Select Six

Sexions
by Renée Sigel

In this deeply evocative début anthology, Renée Sigel takes the reader on a journey through a richly textured labyrinth of truth and contradiction. Her words and imagery delve into the core nature of self - of belonging, of sexuality, of displacement: Five African Songs and Sexions, selections from life and love, alternately weave through the intense and tenacious fabric of the African soul and its convergence with suburban ordinariness. Hottentot Venus traces the tragic true life story of a young woman, Sara Baartman, which mirrors the current reality of the modern day KoiSan tribe.

From continent to continent, Renée Sigel's poetic insights will echo over landscapes and divides.

Sigel's poetry has an erotic thrill and a daring rarely seen in contemporary English language poetry. She is a poet entirely in love with both language and the world, but at the same time absolutely unsentimental about either. ***Kevin Higgins***
Sigel is one whose place in time, love of language, and clarity of eye has produced a poet with work that stands among the best of her generation. ***Roger Humes***

ISBN 978-1-905202-02-7

listen to the geckos singing from a balcony
by tolulope ogunlesi

Tolulope Ogunlesi is a real discovery, a young poet of talent and enormous potential. This is his first collection of poetry.

... witty and engaging; a promising first outing by a poet with a clear, precocious voice. A truly significant achievement. ***Niyi Osundare***
This is one of the most remarkable first collections I have come across ... Tolu's poetry is sturdy, full-blooded and often humorous. ***Gavin Bantock***
This is truly a gifted writer. I now look for everything he writes. ***Kola Boof***
Ogunlesi's value as a poet is not dependent on the drastic need for voices ... Yes, memorable metaphor, a fine ear and strong, live feeling are brought to the task. They also promise an impressive development. ***Judith Rodriguez***
If poetry is a reflection of the soul, then Ogunlesi poems reflect a soul much older than his twenty-one years ... Tolulope tells of the African experience, an echo that translates easily to the African American experience, as well. ***Judith R. Goff***

ISBN 978-1-904492-84-9

Select Six
www.bewrite.net/select_six.htm

Printed in the United States
218893BV00001B/2/P